'*Dear Carice . . .*'

Postcards from Edward Elgar to his daughter

from the archives of
The Elgar Birthplace Museum

OSBORNE
HERITAGE

Published by Osborne Books Limited
Unit 1B Everoak Estate
Bromyard Road
Worcester
WR2 5HN
Tel 01905 748071

Printed by the Bath Press, Bath.

British Library Cataloguing in Publication Data
A catalogue record for this book is available from the British Library.

ISBN 1 872962 66 1

Introduction

This previously unpublished selection of Edward Elgar's postcards to his daughter Carice has been reproduced from an album which previously belonged to her and is now preserved in the archives of The Elgar Birthplace Museum. The earliest postcard in this selection dates from the 1890s and the latest from 1913. They constitute a fascinating Edwardian 'period piece' showing Elgar as composer, traveller and father.

The aim of this book has been to present the postcards in the form of an album of the Edwardian era. The cards appear in chronological order as far as is logically possible and are accompanied by a transcription of what Elgar has written together with notes setting the scene and explaining the text.

Carice Irene Elgar was born on 14 August 1890. Her mother, Alice, was forty years old at the time and Edward was thirty three. Carice's name is derived in a typically quirky Elgarian way from her mother's full name <u>Car</u>oline Al<u>ice</u>; it had been coined by Elgar in 1888 in the dedication to his *Salut d'amour*, written at the time of his engagement.

The face of Carice that looks at us from the photographic archives is not always a happy one, and it is certainly true that the demands of a household which contained a creative 'Genius' (as Elgar was known by a family friend) did not always allow for the noise and disruption inevitably caused by a young child. Carice was sent away to The Mount, a boarding school not so far from her parents' home in Malvern. The Headmistress of The Mount, Rosa Burley, described the young Carice, before she was of school age:

> . . . a very beautiful little girl with flaxen hair and a roseleaf complexion. But the expression on her face troubled me, for it was one of profound sadness. She never smiled or laughed; and when I learned that from the first she had been taught never to make the least noise for fear of disturbing her father, I understood her unnatural look of resignation.

The postcards presented here show Elgar in a different perspective, as a father who was fun-loving and who was prepared to give time to his daughter. He shared Carice's love of animals and sketched a variety of mice, dogs and tadpoles on the cards, a practice he also carried out in correspondence with his friends. Carice later wrote: 'The 'mice' originated in his writing of figures on a cheque; he always put a tail to the final nought, and it was easy to add the ears – *not* on the cheque – but on bits of paper for my amusement as a child.'

The most memorable of Carice's pets, a white angora rabbit named 'Pietro D'Alba' became famous as a dedicatee of the part-song 'Owls' and is named by Elgar as the translator of the words for the song 'The Torch'. Elgar, always the handyman, built a hutch to house Carice's animals. There is reason to suppose that Elgar and Carice identified themselves with certain animals; Elgar certainly signed himself as a fox on letters to friends ('Reynart the Fox' from a book given to him by Ivor Atkins), and Carice became associated with the rabbit (Elgar calls her 'Babbity'). On the postcards appear phrases such as 'Mr Fox is here'and 'Mr Rabbit's swimming bath'.

Carice also helped her father in his many hobbies, including photography. A photograph of Carice in her nightgown is clearly a result of one of their photographic sessions. As she grew older she accompanied him on walks: she was with him in Wales in 1903 when he was orchestrating 'The Apostles' and joined him in Italy in 1904 when a little tune he repeated for her amusement became embodied in his overture *In the South*.

The notes to the postcards help to explain the 'baby-talk' family language used by the Elgars. 'Father' becomes 'Faser' and 'very' is often quoted as 'vesy'. This family language is also used by the parents in correspondence and diary entries.

The postcards themselves are sometimes signed by more than one person. Alice Elgar frequently adds a note, even if it is about the weather. In one case a card written exclusively by Alice has been included here, as it forms a significant part of the sequence of cards from Düsseldorf, written in May 1902, at the time of the second German performance of *The Dream of Gerontius*.

Other friends 'mentioned within' include Henry Ettling and Alfred Rodewald. Ettling, a German wine dealer, is described by Rosa Burley as 'an extraordinary figure, stout, very ugly . . . always jingling sovereigns in his trouser pockets. He loved playing the timpani . . . [and] could entertain the children, grown up and otherwise, with conjuring tricks.' Elgar, who had seen *Parsifal* in 1892, called him 'Uncle Klingsor' on account of his magical powers. Alfred Rodewald, a Liverpool merchant of means who had made his fortune on the Cotton Exchange, was a patron of music and a skilled amateur conductor. Elgar directed his Liverpool Orchestral Society on a number of occasions and was a guest from time-to-time at his cottage at Minafon in North Wales.

The postcards in this album are more than a visual divertimento. They illuminate the life of a working composer with many flashes of humour and humanity and show him to be a caring father as well as a creative musician.

Michael Fardon

Summer 1997

Acknowledgements

Osborne Heritage would like to thank The Elgar Birthplace Trust for granting permission for the reproduction of postcards from the Carice Elgar-Blake album, photographs from the Museum archive and extracts from the Elgar diaries. Particular thanks must go to Melanie Weatherley, Curator, and to Chris Bennett of The Elgar Birthplace Museum, for their help in selecting the cards and for advising on dating and handwriting. Thanks are also due to Anita Sherwood for the book design and to Jon Moore for book production.

Osborne Heritage is particularly indebted to Elgar's godson, E. Wulstan Atkins, for reading the drafts, for helping with the interpretation of Elgar's handwriting and for advising on the text of the book.

Plas Gwyn, Hereford, July 1906

This charming German
Christmas 'postcard' –
captioned 'Merry Christmas' –
is dated 23 December 1901.
The reference to 'Mr Rabbit' is
the first of many in the
collection and in this case is
probably the opening phrase of
a story to be told.

"Now Mr Rabbit, &c."
Sweet dear love
Ed. Elgar

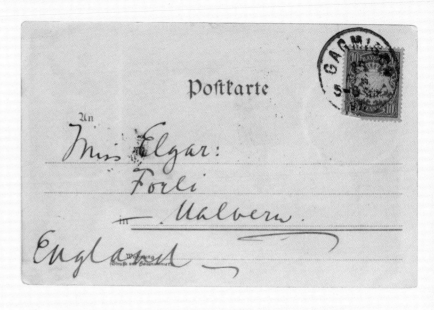

Best birthday wishes from father and mother. Here is a nice little chamois and a Bavarian man. Love E. E.

GRUSS aus PARTENKIRCHEN.

Elgar was staying at Minafon, Rodewald's summer cottage at Bettws-y-coed in North Wales. The card is dated 10 June 1901. The reference to 'Mr. Fox' is part of the animal saga which Elgar constructed, not only for the ten year-old Carice's benefit, but also in correspondence with his friends. Rosa Burley was Headmistress of Carice's school, The Mount, and a family friend. 'Faser' is Elgar 'baby-talk' for 'Father'.

Two years later Carice was to join Elgar at Minafon while he was scoring 'The Apostles'.

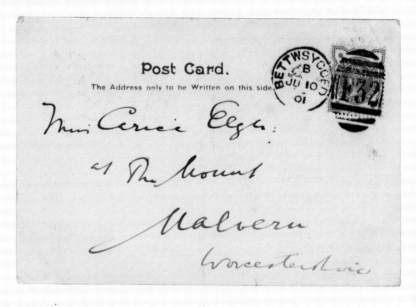

Post Card.

The Address only to be Written on this side.

Mrs Carice Elgar.
at The Mount
Malvern
Worcestershire

Such a lovely place and such different air from Malvern – _so_ sleepy poor Faser is asleep all day which is good for old men. Thank Miss Burley for the Athenaeum Much love, darling. Mr Fox is here. Your Faser

at Ulma from

Bettws-y-coed.

NORTH WALES

Ther 10. 1901

Such a lovely place & such different
air from Malvern — so sleepy here
there is such all day which is
good for old men. Drink Malverley
full Afternoon. Much love, darling
Mr Fox is here. Zuis Foses

NOTES

This card from London is dated 3 May 1902. Although Elgar has signed it and added some mice, the message and address are in the hand of Henry Ettling, known to Carice as 'Uncle Klingsor'. It is addressed to a 'Miss Knott-Gorpidge'. The 'Knott' element is a private joke along the lines of 'You are Miss Elgar, are you (k)nott?'

Among the other signatories to the card are the critic Alfred Kalisch, A J Jaeger ('Nimrod' of The Enigma Variations), Percy Pitt the composer and the conductor Felix Weingartner.

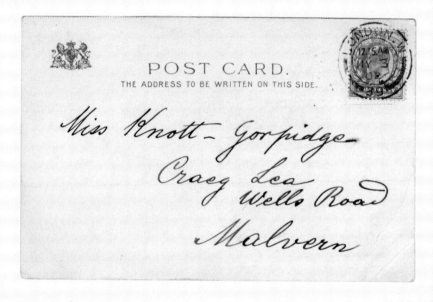

POST CARD.
THE ADDRESS TO BE WRITTEN ON THIS SIDE.

Miss Knott — Gorpidge
Craeg Lea
Wells Road
Malvern

Dearest! We all send you our best love. Uncle Klingsor, A. Kalisch, A. J. Jaeger (Nimrod), Percy Pitt, Alfred [signature not clear] F. Weingartner, C. Halir, Edwd. Elgar.

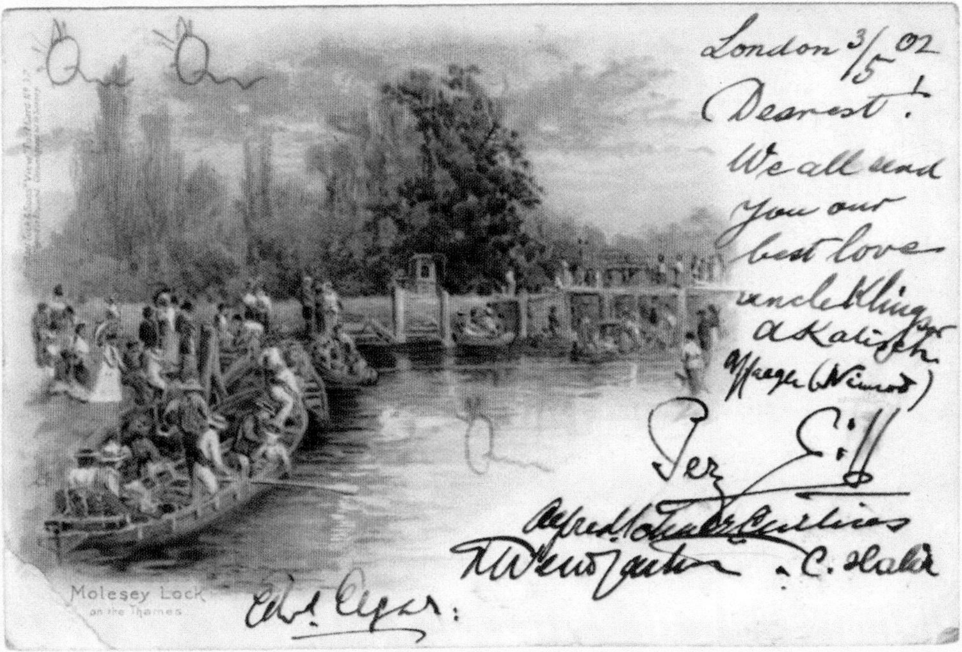

Molesey Lock
on the Thames

London 3/5 02

Dearest!

We all send
you our
best love
uncle Kling
& Kalisch

[signatures]

Ed. Elgar:

The Elgars – but not Carice – had travelled to Düsseldorf with Rodewald to be present at the Lower Rhine Festival performance of 'The Dream of Gerontius' on 19 May 1902.

As this and the next two postcards show, the performance was a welcome triumph after the disastrous first performance in Birmingham in 1900. Carice herself had been present (aged 10) at the Birmingham rehearsal during which Elgar had lost patience at the out-of-key singing of the chorus.

POSTKARTE.

Miss Elgar:
at The Mount
Malvern
England ,

All safe and well. Much love. Mr Tibbert did not come to say good bye. Gerontius is going to be splendid! Wish you were here, much love, your affect[ionate] faser, Ed. Elgar

Städtische Tonhalle.

May 18·02

Gruss aus Düsseldorf

Ah safe &
Oh. much
love.
W. Pibbert
did not come
by proof
bze. Gerontius
is going to be
splendid. O

with yr sere love much

love   your affect. fr'er   Ed. Elgar

Very happy with Mr Rodewald, rehearsal half over, yr affect(ionate) faser. Ed.Elgar.
A E Rodewald with a big kiss.
At rehearsal, Faser cheered & cheered. Yr Aff C.A.E.

DÜSSELDORF
TONHALLENGARTEN.

NOTES

This card was written on 20 May 1902 by Alice Elgar (C.A.E.) the day after the successes of the Düsseldorf 'Gerontius'. The second part of the message (at the sides of the card), with its typically English reference to the weather, is a postscript.

During the supper that evening 'Gerontius' was publicly praised by Richard Strauss who proposed a toast: 'I raise my glass to the welfare and success of the first English Progressivist, Meister Edward Elgar'.

The Elgars travelled with Rodewald on Thursday to Kassel.

POSTKARTE.

Miss Elgar
at The Mount
Malvern
England.

Most splendid evening, be*auti*ful performance & received with _rapture_, Faser shouted for again and again. So glad to have y[ou]r letter. Much love y(ou)r *C.A.E.* Weather _dreadful_. We are to go somewhere on Thursday with Mr Rodewald do not know where. There is a great dinner here today and a great supper to end the festival this evening.

Most splendid evening, beautiful performance & received with

Garten der Tonhalle.

Gruss aus Düsseldorf

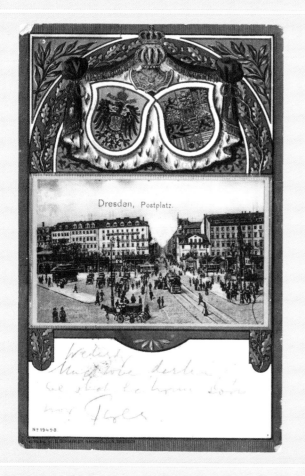

This card is postmarked 28 May 1902. The Elgars were in Dresden, on holiday following the successes of the Lower Rhine Festival performance of 'Gerontius' on 19 May. They had also been to Eisenach, the birthplace of J S Bach.

'Faser' is the Elgar family word for 'father'.

Wednesday. Much love darling, we shall be home soon now, Faser

This card is dated 22 July 1902. Elgar and friends had travelled to the Bayreuth Festival at the invitation of Archibald Ramsden, a piano dealer.

Elgar had recently been practising the trombone, much to Carice's amusement. A vignette of a trombonist is printed on the reverse of the card.

The card is also signed by Henry Ettling (Uncle Klingsor) and the critic Alfred Kalisch.

I hope you will like the trombone player. Very wet weather. Heart's love E. E.

This card is postmarked 28 July 1902. Elgar adds a note of fatherly concern about the cards to Carice signed by the conductor Hans Richter and Siegfried Wagner. (These cards are shown on the following pages).

Elgar, who was already a celebrity in German musical circles, was clearly getting tired of being lionised, largely through the enthusiasm of Henry Ettling (Uncle Klingsor). The type of card Elgar would have signed appears elsewhere in this album, sent to Carice 'to approve of'.

Miss Carice Elgar:
c The Mount
Malvern
England.

You must take great care of the cards sent, by dear Dr. Richter and Siegfried Wagner - who signed one for you. Poor Faser got tired of signing cards for Mr Ettling. Faser had to sign for all sorts of people - some of 'em did not want it I think. So much fuss. Love E. E.

Nürnberg   Ludwigsthor.

Dr. Trenkler Co., Leipzig. 17086

You must take great care of the Cards sent by dear
Dr Miller & Siegfried Wagner. He signed one for you
or three of my misc cards for Mr Epping — presented to him
in all sorts of people — some of 'em did not want it I think so
much fuss. Love. E.P.

BAYREUTH
Das Innere des Opernhauses

This card is postmarked 27 July 1902 and addressed by Alice Elgar (address not shown here). The signatories are Elgar, Hans Richter and Uncle Klingsor (Henry Ettling). The works that Elgar heard at Bayreuth included the first three dramas of 'The Ring', 'The Flying Dutchman' and 'Parsifal'. There would doubtless have been jibes and jokes about the latter in which the character Klingsor appears.

Hans Richter, Edward Elgar, much love, Uncle Klingsor

This card from Bayreuth is postmarked 28 July 1902 and has been autographed by Siegfried Wagner. Elgar had sent a separate card asking Carice to take care of this card and the card, signed by Hans Richter, shown opposite.

Siegfried Wagner.
Best love. E. Elgar.

This card is postmarked 26 July 1902. Elgar returned to England on 29 July to immerse himself in 'The Apostles', which, like the Wagnerian music dramas made prominent use of thematic 'motifs'.

Note the use of the Elgar family word 'vesy' in place of 'very'.

Postkarte.

An

Miss Carice Elgar
1 The Mount

Malvern

England

Saturday. Much love. Coming home vesy soon.
E. Elgar.

GRUSS aus BAYREUTH.

Wagnertheater.

Obere Fontaine & Sonnentempel.

RICHARD WAGNER

Villa Wahnfried

GEB. BECHTOLD & C?
WIESBADEN.

NOTES

This card is postmarked 28 July 1902. Elgar has drawn a 'winged wheel' (a reference to the train) next to his message.

Elgar's concern for his mother, who had been such an influence and support, was well founded. She died on 1 September 1902, just a week before the start of the Worcester Festival. On the Thursday of the Festival, Elgar, dressed in mourning black, conducted a moving performance of 'Gerontius'. A fellow musician wrote 'We were all deeply affected . . . While Elgar was conducting, the tears were running down his cheeks.'

Waiting for the train. Had to start at 6 o'c[lock]. Poor grandmother is so ill. Love hope to see you soon. E. E. I come as fast as the winged wheels will bring me.

NÜRNBERG. Panorama von St. Johannis

KUNSTVERLAG HERMANN MARTIN NÜRNBERG

PASSEPARTOUTKARTE DEP 12386

Writing for the train
Hurst to start at 6 o'c.
poor Grandmother is so
ill. Love to all hope to
see em soon. E. E.

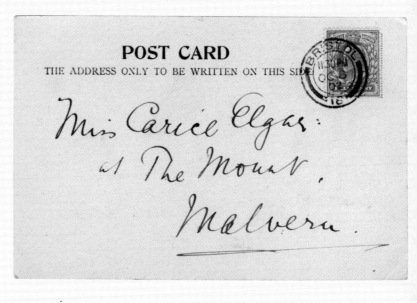

POST CARD
THE ADDRESS ONLY TO BE WRITTEN ON THIS SIDE

Miss Carice Elgar
at The Mount,
Malvern.

Much love, darling Babbity, Jaser, Edward Elgar.

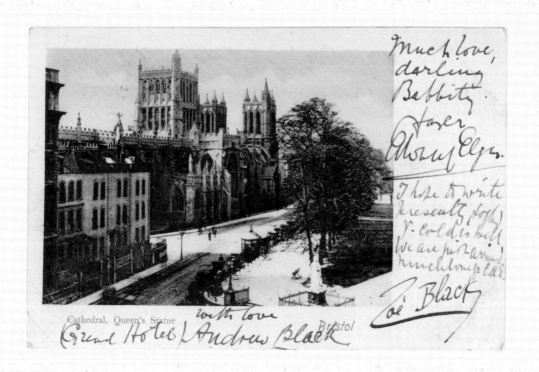

Cathedral, Queen's Statue   Bristol

Much love,
darling
Babbity.
Love
Always Elgar.

I hope to write
presently soft
v. cold to-night.
We are picturing
much love E A E

Zoë Black

with love
(Grand Hotel) Andrew Black

NOTES

This card is postmarked 15 September 1902 and was sent from Liverpool. On the previous day Elgar had conducted a concert of his music at nearby New Brighton. The orchestra was Rodewald's Liverpool Orchestral Society and the works included the 'Enigma Variations', the 'Cockaigne' overture, 'Pomp and Circumstance March' No.1, 'Serenade Mauresque', three of the 'Sea Pictures', and an extract from the 'Grania and Diarmid' incidental music.

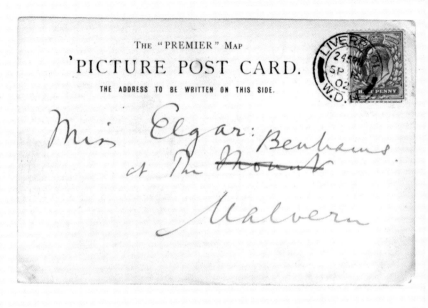

THE "PREMIER" MAP
'PICTURE POST CARD.
THE ADDRESS TO BE WRITTEN ON THIS SIDE.

*Miss Elgar: Benham's.
at The ~~Mount~~
Malvern*

Monday. Much love. Home on Tuesday. Faser.

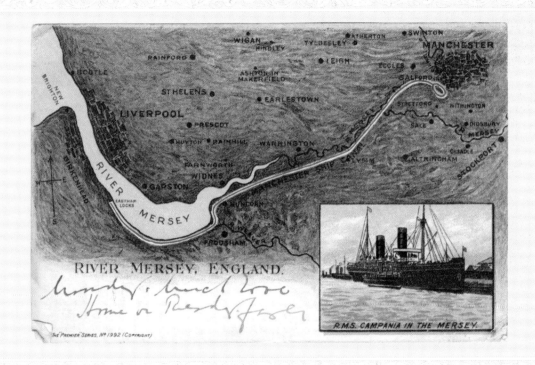

RIVER MERSEY, ENGLAND.

R.M.S. CAMPANIA IN THE MERSEY.

NOTES

This personalised card, dated 30 May 1903, with its quotation from 'Gerontius', was sent to The Mount, the Malvern school to which Carice was sent as a boarder. She was aged twelve at the time. The card was evidently not posted, but this is not surprising, bearing in mind the fact that the school was a short distance away from the Elgar home at Craeg Lea.

The 'Dr. Elgar' citation refers to the honorary doctorate conferred by Cambridge University on 22 November 1900.

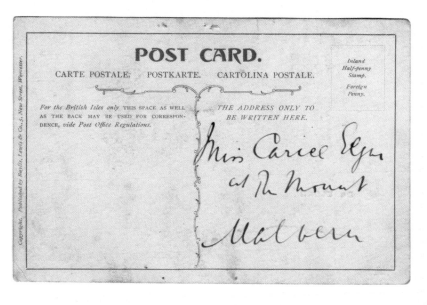

for Carice - a new card sent to me to 'approve of' - but
Carice must approve first!
Edward Elgar.

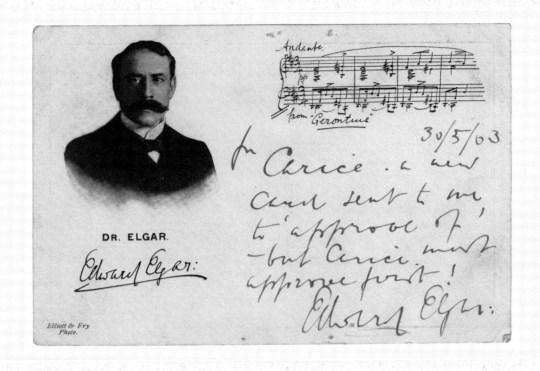

DR. ELGAR.

Edward Elgar:

Andante.

from "Gerontius"

30/5/03

for Carice — a new card sent to me to 'approve of' — but Carice must approve first!

Edward Elgar:

Elliott & Fry
Photo.

NOTES

This card is postmarked 2 July 1903. Elgar was again staying at Minafon, Rodewald's cottage in North Wales and was deeply involved there in the orchestration of 'The Apostles'. Rodewald meantime was speeding up and down the Welsh roads in a novelty of the time – a motor car.

Elgar notes on the card 'Mr Rabbit's swimming bath.'

Carice joined the Elgars at Minafon for the last week of July and went for walks with her father, enjoying the Welsh streams and mountain woodlands.

POST CARD.
THE ADDRESS TO BE WRITTEN ON THIS SIDE.

HALF PENNY

Miss Elgar
4 The Mount
Malvern.

We have just arrived. had a nice journey but very long. We all send love to you, yr affectn. father Ed. Elgar. Mr Rabbit's swimming bath.

Raphael Tuck & Sons' "County" Postcard No. 8122. "DENBIGH". Photograph in Berlin.

Pont-y-pair
BETTWS-Y-COED

Mr Rabbits' swimming bath.

We have just arrived & had a nice journey but very long. We all send love to you Yr affect old fellow Ed. Elgar

NOTES

This card from Bath is postmarked 4 May 1904. Elgar has sketched in two tadpoles ('taddies').

Alice Elgar's diary for the day reads: 'E. explored Bath & then went on to Weston S. Mare. Of course <u>hated it</u> & fled & returned late.'

St Catherine's was the home of Hon. Richard Strutt, a friend of the Elgars. He owned a horse-drawn houseboat in the style of a canal barge which he used to have towed to Worcester and moored on the banks of the River Severn, opposite the Cathedral.

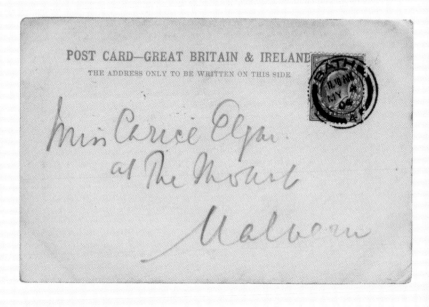

POST CARD—GREAT BRITAIN & IRELAND

THE ADDRESS ONLY TO BE WRITTEN ON THIS SIDE

Mrs Carice Elgar. at The Mount Malvern

The taddies are well. (Bath). Much love. Edw. Elgar.

ST. CATHERINE'S.

(Bath) *Much love.*

3184

NOTES

This card of a Teesdale Mountain stream was posted in Darlington on 22 June 1904.

Elgar was returning from Durham where he had been awarded an honorary doctorate (hence the reference to the doctoral purple).

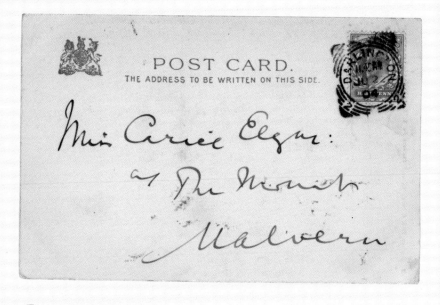

Darlington. On the way home. I wore a lovely purple hood yesterday! Love E.E.

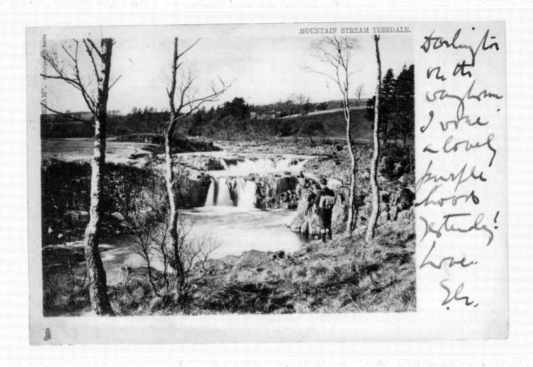

MOUNTAIN STREAM TEESDALE.

Darling,
on the
way home
I wore
a lovely
purple
hood
yesterday!
Love.
Ez.

This card is postmarked 25 May 1904. The Elgars were enjoying German hospitality at the Lower Rhine Festival where Steinbach conducted a successful performance of 'The Apostles'.

The Elgars were evidently steaming up the Rhine on the aptly named Lohengrin.

Elgar has again used the word 'Faser' for 'Father'.

Alice has added a little postscript.

We are with the Chor. Fest. Coming home very soon. Much love Faser.
Lovely day, much love C.A.E.

An Bord des Rheindampfers:

FR. DIETZ, DÜSSELDORF.

Much love. Moglio. Faser

This card from Mainz is postmarked 30 November 1904. Elgar had travelled to the Continent for performances of 'In the South' (in Cologne) and 'The Apostles' in Mainz and at Rotterdam.

Carice was at home with her mother at Plas Gwyn in Hereford.

The comment on the card against the word 'Grüss' (Greetings) is 'Gosh', probably a play on words. Elgar's exclamation 'uks' appears on another card when a vista is seen from a dizzy height.

Gosh, uks! Edward Elgar (love)

Gruss aus Mainz.　　　　　Totalansicht vom Stephansturm.

Gruts!

This card is postmarked 4 December, 1904.

Elgar had travelled from Mainz to the Netherlands to hear 'The Apostles' at Rotterdam.

Elgar was on tour with Frank Schuster. They also visited The Hague and Amsterdam before returning to Germany.

Off to Amsterdam. Love Faser.

Een hollandsche Groet

LONDON. Nelsons Column.

Just back from palsol.
Al vesy nice your own F&M
July 5: 04

Elgar was knighted on 5 July 1904. Alice records in her diary (note the family language): ' E. dessed & looked vesy booful. A. helped him & buckled his sword. Then Frank [Elgar's brother] arrived & drove to Buckingham Palace with E. & then met A. & went shopping with her. Returned & found E. arrived. The King smiled charmingly & said 'Very pleased to see you here Sir Edward."

Just back from Palace. All vesy nice, your own Faser. July 5: 04.

The Elgars set sail for New York aboard the Deutschland on 9 June 1905. They posted the card on the ship. Alice has added 'Sea smooth, huge ship, hardly any motion. Thursday D.V. in New York. Thinking of you both & our love. Should arrive D.V. on Thursday.'

They arrived in New York on 15 June for a four week tour, in torrid heat, visiting Yale and Boston.

At sea. All well.
much love Faser.

NOTES

This card of Llangollen, North Wales, is postmarked 25 August 1905. The mention of 'Peter' is undoubtedly a reference to Pietro d'Alba, Carice's white angora rabbit.

Elgar may have been on a short trip to North Wales as he was back in Hereford on 25 August to entertain Ivor Atkins and to play through passages from a part-song 'Evening Scene'. This composition was based on Coventry Patmore's poem 'The River'. Elgar's love of the riverside, and particularly at that time of the Wye, is reflected in this postcard of the River Dee.

This is very nice. I wish Peter were here.

LLANGOLLEN, THE BRIDGE.

Elgar had conducted a number of his works at the May Cincinnati Festival where he was described by 'The Cincinnati Post' as 'a tall, spare figure in ice-cream clothes . . . the typical Englishman, silent, reserved and unsocial – until after dinner.' He was enthusiastically received, but he found the American audience's habit of clapping after every scene of 'The Apostles' a little unsettling.

The card from Cincinnati Zoo is postmarked 18 May 1906; it was posted in New York, on the day he set sail for England.

Home soon. Love Faser.

CINCINNATI (Ohio). - At the Zoo

In March and April 1907 Elgar went on another American tour. This card, postmarked 7 April, is from Chicago, where, he conducted works including 'Enigma Varaiations' and 'In the South'. According to the local press his beat on the rostrum was 'the long straight beat of the British bandmaster ... He stands with feet well apart and with body noticeably bent at the hips.'

It is known that Elgar was not happy with the choice of accommodation – Chicago's best, but also its largest and possibly its noisiest hotel.

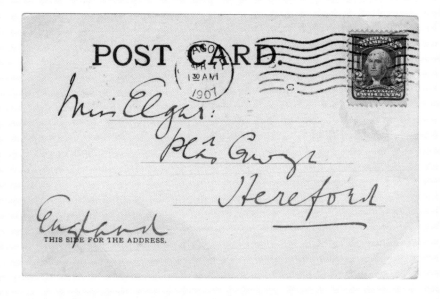

Could no other area? My cake is dough. Oh! this place. My child. Love Faser.

AUDITORIUM HOTEL AND ANNEX, CHICAGO

Could as other som'd my cake is dough.
Oh! this place. my child: love Stores

No. 166. V. O. Hammon Pub. Co., Chicago

Souvenir de: Les chiens des rues.

Constantinople. I love these poor wows. [signature]

Editeur Max Fruchtermann, Constantinople. 1521   Phot. Abdullah.

In September 1905 Elgar and his brother Frank were entertained aboard HMS Surprise as guests of the British Mediterranean Fleet. They sailed around the Greek islands to Turkey, where they made their way by Austrian steamer to Constantinople (Istanbul), arriving on 25 September. This card shows 'poor wows', which is Elgar language for dogs ('bow wows').

Constantinople. I love these poor wows. Faser

Another card from Stamboul (Istanbul) sent in the last week of September 1905.

Elgar's diary shows the impact made by this East-West gateway of cultures: 'Glorious sunrise & the minarets of Stamboul began to come through the mist — wonderful . . . Drove up to the higher part for views: in the sunset the Bosphorus & Stamboul were insanely beautiful.'

Stamboul. Love from Jaser.

Marchand d'eau.

Souvenir de Stamboul

Editeur Max Fruchtermann, Constantinople. 1509

Phot. Sébah & Joaillier.

This card is postmarked 7 March 1913. Elgar had suffered from poor health for a number of years and had taken short recuperative holidays in the spa town of Llandrindod Wells, Wales. It is known that he was there twice in February 1909, the first visit proving more successful than the second.

In this card from the Gwalia Hotel, where he stayed from 4 to 11 March, Elgar has indicated his room and characteristically drawn dogs on the roof. Carice was 22 at the time.

The card has been sent to Severn House, the Elgars' London home.

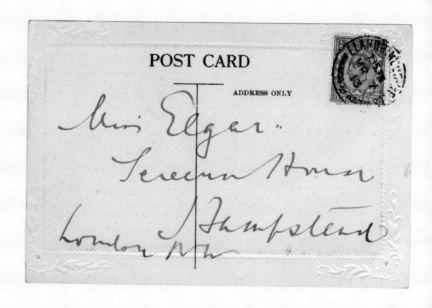

my room

Gwalia Hotel, Llandrindod Wells.

Telephone 40 P. O.　　　　　Telegraphic Gwalia.

Birchwood, 3 August 1900